Presented to:

_____

From:

_____

Date:

_____

D1435810

GodSpeaks™
Promises for Living

Honor Books
Tulsa, Oklahoma

GodSpeaks™ Promises for Living
ISBN 1-56292-664-0
Copyright © 2001 by Honor Books
P.O. Box 55388
Tulsa, Oklahoma 74155

Printed in the United States of America. All rights reserved under International Copyright Law. Contents and/or cover may not be reproduced in whole or in part in any form without the express written consent of the Publisher.

The trademark GodSpeaks™ is used by permission pursuant to a license obtained from GodSpeaks™, Inc., and may not be otherwise used without the consent of GodSpeaks™, Inc. All rights reserved.

The original GodSpeaks™ Messages © 2000 GodSpeaks™, Inc. All rights reserved.

Let's meet at my house Sunday before the game.

C'mon over and bring the kids.

What part of "Thou Shalt Not"
didn't you understand?

We need to talk.

Keep using my name in vain,
I'll make rush hour longer.

Loved the wedding! Invite me to the marriage.

That "Love Thy Neighbor" thing … I meant that.

I love you. I love you. I love you.

Will the road you're on get you to my place?

Follow me.

Need directions?

You think it's hot here?

Tell the kids I love them.

Need a marriage counselor? I'm available.

Have you read my #1 bestseller?
(There will be a test.)

Do you have any idea where you're going?

"Big Bang Theory"? You've got to be kidding.

My way *is* the highway.

References

Unless otherwise indicated, all Scripture quotations are taken from the *Holy Bible, New International Version* ®. NIV ®. Copyright © 1973, 1978, 1984 by International Bible Society. Used by permission of Zondervan Publishing House. All rights reserved.

Scripture quotations marked KJV are taken from the *King James Version* of the Bible.

Scripture quotations marked AMP are taken from *The Amplified Bible. Old Testament* copyright © 1965, 1987 by Zondervan Corporation, Grand Rapids, Michigan. *New Testament* copyright © 1958, 1987 by The Lockman Foundation, La Habra, California. Used by permission.

Scripture quotations marked TLB are taken from *The Living Bible* © 1971. Used by permission of Tyndale House Publishers, Inc., Wheaton, Illinois 60189. All rights reserved.

Scripture quotations marked NKJV are taken from *The New King James Version.* Copyright © 1979, 1980, 1982, 1988, 1994, Thomas Nelson, Inc.

Scripture quotations marked CEV are taken from the *Contemporary English Version,* copyright © 1991, 1992, 1995 by the American Bible Society. Used by permission.

Scripture quotations marked NASB are taken from the *New American Standard Bible.* Copyright © The Lockman Foundation 1960, 1962, 1963, 1968, 1971, 1972, 1973, 1975, 1977, 1995. Used by permission.

Scripture quotations marked NCV are quoted from *The Holy Bible, New Century Version,* copyright © 1987, 1988, 1991 by Word Publishing, Dallas, Texas 75039. Used by permission.

Scripture quotations marked TEV are from the *Today's English Version—Second Edition* © 1992 by American Bible Society. Used by permission.

Scripture quotations marked NLT are taken from the *Holy Bible, New Living Translation,* copyright ©1996. Used by permission of Tyndale House Publishers, Inc., Wheaton, Illinois 60189. All right reserved.

Scripture quotations marked RSV are taken from *The Revised Standard Version Bible.* Copyright © 1946. *Old Testament* section copyright © 1952 by the Division of Christian Education of the Churches of Christ in the United States of America. Used by permission.

Scripture quotations marked THE MESSAGE are taken from *The Message,* copyright © by Eugene H. Peterson, 1993, 1994, 1995, 1996. Used by permission of NavPress Publishing Group.

Introduction

God has a lot to say, and He has said it pretty plainly within the framework of the Bible. But, despite the fact that the Bible is one of the best known and most widely read books on the planet, most people really aren't familiar with how its concepts and principles fit into their everyday lives.

If you are one of those people, this book has been designed especially for you. The statements attributed to God are, of course, not His actual words. They are, however, statements that illustrate principles He teaches in the Bible. We hope that they will cause you to meditate on God's character, question some of your preconceived notions, and discover for yourself the personal nature of His love and care for you.

We also hope you will be inspired and encouraged by the scriptures and amused by this unabashed approach. If you have questions or would like to make comments, please feel free to contact us at our website: www.GodSpeaks.org.

Table of Contents

Encouragement

Prayer

God's Nature

Words of Wisdom

Encouragement

Got Questions? I'm the Answer
—God

Let's talk.
—GOD

If you want to know what God wants you to do, ask him, and he will gladly tell you, for he is always ready to give a bountiful supply of wisdom to all who ask him; he will not resent it.

James 1:5 TLB

Call to me and I will answer you and tell you great and unsearchable things you do not know.

Jeremiah 33:3

The Lord pleads with you still: Ask where the good road is, the godly paths you used to walk in, in the days of long ago. Travel there, and you will find rest for your souls.

Jeremiah 6:16 TLB

Behold, I stand at the door and knock. If anyone hears My voice and opens the door, I will come in to him and dine with him, and he with Me.

Revelation 3:20 NKJV

Loved the wedding! Invite me to the marriage.

—GOD

For this reason a man will leave his father and mother and be united to his wife, and they will become one flesh.

Genesis 2:24

And the Lord God said, "It is not good that man should be alone; I will make him a helper comparable to him."

Genesis 2:18 NKJV

❧

Jesus said to them . . . "But from the beginning of creation, 'God made them male and female.' 'For this reason a man shall leave his father and mother and be joined to his wife, and the two shall become one.' So they are no longer two but one. What therefore God has joined together, let not man put asunder."

Mark 10:5-9 RSV

❧

The husband should fulfill his marital duty to his wife, and likewise the wife to her husband.

1 Corinthians 7:3

Follow me.

—GOD

*"I am the world's Light. No one
who follows me stumbles around
in the darkness. I provide plenty
of light to live in."*

John 8:12 THE MESSAGE

"If any man serve me, let him follow me; and where I am, there shall also my servant be: if any man serve me, him will my Father honour."

John 12:26 KJV

❧

"If anyone would come after me, he must deny himself and take up his cross and follow me. For whoever wants to save his life will lose it, but whoever loses his life for me will find it."

Matthew 16:24-25

❧

This suffering is all part of the work God has given you. Christ, who suffered for you, is your example. Follow in his steps.

1 Peter 2:21 TLB

Let's meet at my house Sunday before the game.

—GOD

Let's see how inventive we can be in encouraging love and helping out, not avoiding worshiping together as some do but spurring each other on, especially as we see the big Day approaching.

Hebrews 10:25 THE MESSAGE

Obey your leaders and submit to their authority. They keep watch over you as men who must give an account. Obey them so that their work will be a joy, not a burden, for that would be of no advantage to you.

Hebrews 13:17

They devoted themselves to the apostles' teaching and to the fellowship, to the breaking of bread and to prayer.

Acts 2:42

Every day they continued to meet together in the temple courts. They broke bread in their homes and ate together with glad and sincere hearts, praising God and enjoying the favor of all the people.

Acts 2:46-47

Don't fear the future. I'm already there.
—GOD

"For I know the plans I have for you," declares the LORD, "plans to prosper you and not to harm you, plans to give you hope and a future."

Jeremiah 29:11

There is surely a future hope for you, and your hope will not be cut off.

Proverbs 23:18

∽

Dear friends, now we are children of God, and what we will be has not yet been made known. But we know that when he appears, we shall be like him, for we shall see him as he is.

1 John 3:2

∽

The plans of the LORD stand firm forever, the purposes of his heart through all generations.

Psalm 33:11

Do I have an offer for you!

—GOD

And this is the promise that he hath promised us, even eternal life.

1 John 2:25 KJV

Command those who are rich in this present world . . . to put their hope in God, who richly provides us with everything for our enjoyment.

1 Timothy 6:17

The Spirit itself beareth witness with our spirit, that we are the children of God: And if children, then heirs; heirs of God, and joint-heirs with Christ; if so be that we suffer with him, that we may be also glorified together.

Romans 8:16,17 KJV

For all the promises of God in him are yea, and in him Amen, unto the glory of God by us.

2 Corinthians 1:20 KJV

I build great homes.

—GOD

Now we know that if the earthly tent we live in is destroyed, we have a building from God, an eternal house in heaven, not built by human hands.

2 Corinthians 5:1

"Do not let your hearts be troubled. Trust in God; trust also in me. In my Father's house are many rooms; if it were not so, I would have told you. I am going there to prepare a place for you. And if I go and prepare a place for you, I will come back and take you to be with me that you also may be where I am. You know the way to the place where I am going."

John 14:1-4

You also, like living stones, are being built into a spiritual house to be a holy priesthood, offering spiritual sacrifices acceptable to God through Jesus Christ.

1 Peter 2:5

In him the whole building is joined together and rises to become a holy temple in the Lord. And in him you too are being built together to become a dwelling in which God lives by his Spirit.

Ephesians 2:21-22

Give me your worries. I'll be up all night anyway.

—GOD

He will never let me stumble,
slip or fall. For he is always
watching, never sleeping.

Psalm 121:3-4 TLB

Casting all your care upon him; for he careth for you.

1 Peter 5:7 KJV

Thou wilt keep him in perfect peace, whose mind is stayed on thee: because he trusteth in thee.

Isaiah 26:3 KJV

I will both lay me down in peace, and sleep: for thou, LORD, only makest me dwell in safety.

Psalm 4:8 KJV

Feeling down?
Just look up.
—GOD

*We have troubles all around us,
but we are not defeated. We do
not know what to do, but we do
not give up the hope of living.
We are persecuted, but God does
not leave us. . . . So we do not
give up.*

2 Corinthians 4:8-9,16 NCV

*Cast your burden upon the L*ORD*, and He will sustain you; He will never allow the righteous to be shaken.*

Psalm 55:22 NASB

❧

My mouth would encourage you; comfort from my lips would bring you relief.

Job 16:5

❧

May our Lord Jesus Christ Himself and God our Father, who has loved us and given us eternal comfort and good hope by grace, comfort and strengthen your hearts in every good work and word.

2 Thessalonians 2:16-17 NASB

Got grace?

—GOD

"My grace is sufficient for thee: for my strength is made perfect in weakness."

2 Corinthians 12:9 KJV

Grace and peace be yours in abundance through the knowledge of God and of Jesus our Lord.

2 Peter 1:2

For if, by the trespass of the one man, death reigned through that one man, how much more will those who receive God's abundant provision of grace and of the gift of righteousness reign in life through the one man, Jesus Christ.

Romans 5:17

From the fullness of his grace we have all received one blessing after another.

John 1:16

It's not too late to be what you might have been.

—GOD

Forget the former things; do not dwell on the past. . . . I am making a way in the desert and streams in the wasteland.

Isaiah 43:18-19

Therefore if any man be in Christ, he is a new creature: old things are passed away; behold, all things are become new.

2 Corinthians 5:17 KJV

I will give you a new heart and put a new spirit in you; I will remove from you your heart of stone and give you a heart of flesh. And I will put my Spirit in you and move you to follow my decrees and be careful to keep my laws.

Ezekiel 36:26-27

Do not conform any longer to the pattern of this world, but be transformed by the renewing of your mind. Then you will be able to test and approve what God's will is—his good, pleasing and perfect will.

Romans 12:2

You look like you could use a faith-lift.

—GOD

And now just as you trusted Christ to save you, trust him, too, for each day's problems; live in vital union with him.

Colossians 2:6 TLB

We live by faith, not by sight.

2 Corinthians 5:7

What is faith? It is the confident assurance that something we want is going to happen. It is the certainty that what we hope for is waiting for us, even though we cannot see it up ahead.

Hebrews 11:1 TLB

"I tell you the truth, anyone who has faith in me will do what I have been doing. He will do even greater things than these, because I am going to the Father."

John 14:12

I make happy endings.

—GOD

We know that all things work together for good to them that love God, to them who are the called according to his purpose.

Romans 8:28 KJV

We are able to hold our heads high no matter what happens and know that all is well, for we know how dearly God loves us, and we feel this warm love everywhere within us because God has given us the Holy Spirit to fill our hearts with his love.

Romans 5:5 TLB

Then maidens will dance and be glad, young men and old as well. I will turn their mourning into gladness; I will give them comfort and joy instead of sorrow.

Jeremiah 31:13

Fear not; you will no longer live in shame. The shame of your youth and the sorrows of widowhood will be remembered no more.

Isaiah 54:4 TLB

Remember your sins? I forgot them.
—GOD

*I will forgive their wickedness
and will remember their sins
no more.*

Hebrews 8:12

As far as the east is from the west, so far has he removed our transgressions from us.

Psalm 103:12

〜

[The LORD declares]: "I am the One who forgives all your sins, for my sake; I will not remember your sins."

Isaiah 43:25 NCV

〜

If we confess our sins, he is faithful and just to forgive us our sins, and to cleanse us from all unrighteousness.

1 John 1:9 KJV

I still create rainbows.

—GOD

I have set my rainbow in the clouds, and it will be the sign of the covenant between me and the earth.

Genesis 9:13

Whenever I bring clouds over the earth and the rainbow appears in the clouds, I will remember my covenant between me and you and all living creatures of every kind.

Genesis 9:14-15

He remembers his covenant forever, the word he commanded, for a thousand generations.

Psalm 105:8

I will make a covenant of peace with them; it will be an everlasting covenant. I will establish them and increase their numbers, and I will put my sanctuary among them forever.

Ezekiel 37:26

I made you, and I don't make mistakes.

—GOD

*God has made us what we are.
In Christ Jesus, God made us to
do good works, which God
planned in advance for us to live
our lives doing.*

Ephesians 2:10 NCV

You created my inmost being; you knit me together in my mother's womb. I praise you because I am fearfully and wonderfully made.

Psalm 139:13-14

For he chose us in him before the creation of the world to be holy and blameless in his sight.

Ephesians 1:4

O L<small>ORD</small>, you have searched me and you know me. You know when I sit and when I rise; you perceive my thoughts from afar. You discern my going out and my lying down; you are familiar with all my ways.

Psalm 139:1-3

Courage is fear that has said its prayers.

—GOD

Be strong, and let your heart take courage, All you who hope in the LORD.

Psalm 31:24 NASB

*Yes, be bold and strong! Banish fear and doubt!
For remember, the Lord your God is with you
wherever you go.*

Joshua 1:9 TLB

*Be strong and courageous, do not be afraid or
tremble . . . for the LORD your God is the one
who goes with you. He will not fail you or
forsake you.*

Deuteronomy 31:6 NASB

*Don't be afraid, for I am with you. Do not be
dismayed, for I am your God. I will strengthen
you. I will help you. I will uphold you with my
victorious right hand.*

Isaiah 41:10 NLT

I love to hear you laugh.

—GOD

He will yet fill your mouth with laughter and your lips with shouts of joy.

Job 8:21

Be happy, young man, while you are young, and let your heart give you joy in the days of your youth.

Ecclesiastes 11:9

❧

No wonder we are happy in the Lord! For we are trusting him. We trust his holy name.

Psalm 33:21 TLB

❧

The joy of the LORD is your strength.

Nehemiah 8:10

Alone you can't. Together we can.
—GOD

"With God all things are possible."
Matthew 19:26

With God's help we shall do mighty things, for he will trample down our foes.

Psalm 60:12 TLB

Now thanks be to God who always leads us in triumph in Christ, and through us diffuses the fragrance of His knowledge in every place.

2 Corinthians 2:14 NKJV

If God is for us, who can be against us? He who did not spare his own Son, but gave him up for us all—how will he not also, along with him, graciously give us all things?

Romans 8:31-32

I'm listening.
—GOD

You will call upon me and come and pray to me, and I will listen to you.

Jeremiah 29:12

If my people, who are called by my name, will humble themselves and pray and seek my face and turn from their wicked ways, then will I hear from heaven and will forgive their sin and will heal their land.

2 Chronicles 7:14

This is the confidence that we have in him, that, if we ask any thing according to his will, he heareth us: And if we know that he hear us, whatsoever we ask, we know that we have the petitions that we desired of him.

1 John 5:14-15 KJV

The righteous cry out, and the LORD hears them; he delivers them from all their troubles.

Psalm 34:17

Prayer

Your secret's safe with me.

—GOD

Blessed is the man who trusts in the LORD*, whose confidence is in him.*

Jeremiah 17:7

Have faith in the LORD your God and you will be upheld.

2 Chronicles 20:20

Let us then approach the throne of grace with confidence, so that we may receive mercy and find grace to help us in our time of need.

Hebrews 4:16

I CRIED unto the LORD with my voice; with my voice unto the LORD did I make my supplication. I poured out my complaint before him; I shewed before him my trouble.

Psalm 142:1-2 KJV

Relax.
I'm in control.
—GOD

I will both lay me down in peace, and sleep: for thou, LORD, only makest me dwell in safety.

Psalm 4:8 KJV

Do not be anxious about anything, but in everything, by prayer and petition, with thanksgiv-
ing, present your requests to God.

Philippians 4:6

∿

Thou wilt keep him in perfect peace, whose
mind is stayed on thee: because he trusteth
in thee.

Isaiah 26:3 KJV

∿

Fear thou not; for I am with thee: be not
dismayed; for I am thy God: I will strengthen
thee; yea, I will help thee; yea, I will uphold
thee with the right hand of my righteousness.

Isaiah 41:10 KJV

Are you talking to me?
—GOD

Call to me and I will answer you and tell you great and unsearchable things you do not know.

Jeremiah 33:3

The eyes of the Lord watch over those who do right, and his ears are open to their prayers.

1 Peter 3:12 NLT

When good people pray, the Lord listens.

Proverbs 15:29 TEV

"Believe that you have received the things you ask for in prayer, and God will give them to you."

Mark 11:24 NCV

Miss you.

—GOD

Here I am! I stand at the door and knock. If anyone hears my voice and opens the door, I will come in and eat with him, and he with me.

Revelation 3:20

You turned away from God, your Creator; you forgot the Mighty Rock, the source of your life.

Deuteronomy 32:18 CEV

❧

Now in Christ Jesus you who once were far away have been brought near through the blood of Christ.

Ephesians 2:13

❧

You will seek me and find me when you seek me with all your heart.

Jeremiah 29:13

Need a lifeline?
—GOD

*Many are the afflictions of
the righteous: but the LORD
delivereth him out of them all.*

Psalm 34:19 KJV

The righteous *cry, and the* LORD *heareth, and delivereth them out of all their troubles.*

Psalm 34:17 KJV

❧

He will deliver the needy who cry out, the afflicted who have no one to help.

Psalm 72:12

❧

God is our refuge and strength, an ever-present help in trouble.

Psalm 46:1

What's your hurry?
—GOD

Be still, and know that I am God.

Psalm 46:10

Be patient and wait for the Lord to act; don't be worried about those who prosper or those who succeed in their evil plans.

Psalm 37:7 TEV

But they that wait upon the LORD shall renew their strength; they shall mount up with wings as eagles; they shall run, and not be weary; and they shall walk, and not faint.

Isaiah 40:31 KJV

Wait on the LORD: be of good courage, and he shall strengthen thine heart: wait, I say, on the LORD.

Psalm 27:14 KJV

Knees knocking?
Try kneeling
on them.

—GOD

My flesh and my heart may fail,
But God is the strength of my
heart and my portion forever.

Psalm 73:26 NASB

God hath not given us the spirit of fear; but of power, and of love, and of a sound mind.

2 Timothy 1:7 KJV

❧

Let us be bold, then, and say, "The Lord is my helper, I will not be afraid. What can anyone do to me?"

Hebrews 13:6 TEV

❧

But when I am afraid, I will put my confidence in you. Yes, I will trust the promises of God. And since I am trusting him, what can mere man do to me?

Psalm 56:3-4 TLB

Planning for your future? I am.

—GOD

"For I know the plans I have for you," declares the LORD, "plans to prosper you and not to harm you, plans to give you hope and a future."

Jeremiah 29:11

There is surely a future hope for you, and your hope will not be cut off.

Proverbs 23:18

No eye has seen, no ear has heard, no mind has conceived what God has prepared for those who love him.

1 Corinthians 2:9

The plans of the LORD stand firm forever, the purposes of his heart through all generations.

Psalm 33:11

Pssst . . . up here!
—GOD

The LORD looks down from heaven on the sons of men to see if there are any who understand, any who seek God.

Psalm 14:2

*You will seek me and find me when you seek
me with all your heart.*

Jeremiah 29:13

❧

*I love them that love me; and those that seek
me early shall find me.*

Proverbs 8:17 KJV

❧

*Let us fix our eyes on Jesus, the author and
perfecter of our faith, who for the joy set before
him endured the cross, scorning its shame, and
sat down at the right hand of the throne of
God. Consider him who endured such opposi-
tion from sinful men, so that you will not grow
weary and lose heart.*

Hebrews 12:2-3

My line is never busy.

—GOD

The Lord is watching his children, listening to their prayers.

1 Peter 3:12 TLB

Even before they finish praying to me, I will answer their prayers.

Isaiah 65:24 TEV

The eyes of the Lord watch over those who do right, and his ears are open to their prayers.

1 Peter 3:12 NLT

Call unto me, and I will answer thee, and shew thee great and mighty things, which thou knowest not.

Jeremiah 33:3 KJV

I'm just a prayer away.

—GOD

Be joyful in hope, patient in affliction, faithful in prayer.

Romans 12:12

When good people pray, the Lord listens.

Proverbs 15:29 TEV

❧

The earnest prayer of a righteous person has great power and wonderful results.

James 5:16 NLT

❧

"All things, whatsoever ye shall ask in prayer, believing, ye shall receive."

Matthew 21:22 KJV

I was—I am—
I always will be.
—GOD

I the LORD do not change.

Malachi 3:6

He said to me: *"It is done. I am the Alpha and the Omega, the Beginning and the End. To him who is thirsty I will give to drink without cost from the spring of the water of life."*

Revelation 21:6

❧

Stand up and praise the LORD *your God, who is from everlasting to everlasting.*

Nehemiah 9:5

❧

The eternal God is your refuge, and underneath are the everlasting arms.

Deuteronomy 33:27

God's Nature

"Big Bang Theory"? You've got to be kidding.

—GOD

By faith—by believing God—we know that the world and the stars—in fact, all things—were made at God's command; and that they were all made from things that can't be seen.

Hebrews 11:3 TLB

*Through him all things were made; without him
nothing was made that has been made. In him
was life, and that life was the light of men.*

John 1:3-4

*By the word of the LORD were the heavens
made, their starry host by the breath of his
mouth. He gathers the waters of the sea into
jars; he puts the deep into storehouses. Let all
the earth fear the LORD; let all the people of the
world revere him. For he spoke, and it came to
be; he commanded, and it stood firm.*

Psalm 33:6-9

*Worthy art thou, our Lord and God, to receive
glory and honor and power, for thou didst
create all things, and by thy will they existed
and were created.*

Revelation 4:11 RSV

Tell the kids
I love them.

—GOD

*"I will be a Father to you,
and you will be my sons
and daughters," says the
Lord Almighty.*

2 Corinthians 6:18

Yet to all who received him, to those who believed in his name, he gave the right to become children of God—children born not of natural descent, nor of human decision or a husband's will, but born of God

John 1:12-13

The Spirit himself testifies with our spirit that we are God's children.

Romans 8:16

How great is the love the Father has lavished on us, that we should be called children of God! And that is what we are! The reason the world does not know us is that it did not know him.

1 John 3:1

Darwin says to tell you he was wrong.

—GOD

It is I who made the earth and created mankind upon it. My own hands stretched out the heavens; I marshaled their starry hosts.

Isaiah 45:12

God created man in his own image, in the image of God he created him; male and female he created them.

Genesis 1:27

Is this the way you repay the LORD, O foolish and unwise people? Is he not your Father, your Creator, who made you and formed you?

Deuteronomy 32:6

Ask now about the former days, long before you time, from the day God created man on the earth; ask from one end of the heavens to the other. Has anything so great as this ever happened, or has anything like it ever been heard of?

Deuteronomy 4:32

Remember that pretty sunset? I painted it just for you.

—GOD

The heavens declare the glory of God; the skies proclaim the work of his hands.

Psalm 19:1

He has made everything beautiful in its time.

Ecclesiastes 3:11

Of old hast thou laid the foundation of the earth:
and the heavens are the work of they hands.

Psalm 102:25 KJV

You alone are the LORD. You made the heavens,
even the highest heavens, and all their starry
host, the earth and all that is on it, the seas and
all that is in them. You give life to everything,
and the multitudes of heaven worship you.

Nehemiah 9:6

Wanna play "Follow the Leader"?

—GOD

"I have set you an example that you should do as I have done."

John 13:15

To this you were called, because Christ suffered for you, leaving you an example, that you should follow in his steps.

1 Peter 2:21

❧

Follow my example, as I follow the example of Christ.

1 Corinthians 11:1

❧

Join with others in following my example, brothers, and take note of those who live according to the pattern we gave you.

Philippians 3:17

Let's do life.

—GOD

Got Questions? I'm the Answer
–God

"I have come that they may have life, and that they may have it more abundantly."

John 10:10 NKJV

My son, do not forget my teaching, but keep my commands in your heart, for they will prolong your life many years and bring you prosperity.

Proverbs 3:1-2

❧

"The Spirit gives life; the flesh counts for nothing. The words I have spoken to you are spirit and they are life."

John 6:63

❧

Jesus said to her, "I am the resurrection and the life. He who believes in me will live, even though he dies; and whoever lives and believes in me will never die. Do you believe this?"

John 11:25-26

Words of Wisdom

Got Questions? I'm the Answer
–God

C'mon over and bring the kids.

—GOD

Jesus said, "Let the little children come to me, and do not hinder them, for the kingdom of heaven belongs to such as these."

Matthew 19:14

Train up a child in the way he should go: and when he is old, he will not depart from it.

Proverbs 22:6 KJV

These commandments that I give you today are to be upon your hearts. Impress them on your children. Talk about them when you sit at home and when you walk along the road, when you lie down and when you get up.

Deuteronomy 6:6-7

All your children shall be taught by the Lord, And great shall be the peace of your children.

Isaiah 54:13 NKJV

My way is the highway.

—GOD

For the LORD God is a sun and shield; the LORD bestows favor and honor; no good thing does he withhold from those whose walk is blameless.

Psalm 84:11

As the heavens are higher than the earth, so are my ways higher than your ways and my thoughts than your thoughts.

Isaiah 55:9

Righteous art thou, O LORD, and upright are thy judgments. Thy testimonies that thou hast commanded are righteous and very faithful.

Psalm 119:137-138 KJV

Trust in the Lord will all your heart, And lean not on your own understanding; In all your ways acknowledge Him, And He shall direct your paths.

Proverbs 3:5-6 NKJV

Have you read my #1 best-seller? (There will be a test.) —GOD

This Book of the Law shall not depart from your mouth, but you shall meditate in it day and night, that you may observe to do according to all that is written in it. For then you will make your way prosperous, and then you will have good success.

Joshua 1:8 NKJV

Your word is a lamp to my feet and a light for my path.

Psalm 119:105

❧

For the Word that God speaks is alive and full of power [making it active, operative, energizing, and effective]; it is sharper than any two-edged sword, penetrating to the dividing line of the breath of life (soul) and [the immortal] spirit, and of joints and marrow [of the deepest parts of our nature], exposing and sifting and analyzing and judging the very thoughts and purposes of the heart.

Hebrews 4:12 AMP

❧

The law of the LORD is perfect, reviving the soul. The statutes of the LORD are trustworthy, making wise the simple. The precepts of the LORD are right, giving joy to the heart. The commands of the LORD are radiant, giving light to the eyes.

Psalm 19:7-8

What part of "Thou Shalt Not" didn't you understand?

—GOD

The statutes of the LORD are right, rejoicing the heart; The commandment of the LORD is pure, enlightening the eyes.

Psalm 19:8 NKJV

*You have laid down precepts that are to be
fully obeyed.*

Psalm 119:4

⟨∾⟩

Thou shalt have no other gods before me.

Exodus 20:3 KJV

⟨∾⟩

*You must not murder. You must not commit
adultery. You must not steal. You must not lie.
You must not be envious of your neighbor's
house, or want to sleep with his wife.*

Exodus 20:13-17 TLB

Keep using my name in vain, I'll make rush hour even longer.

—GOD

You shall not misuse the name of the LORD your God, for the LORD will not hold anyone guiltless who misuses his name.

Exodus 20:7

"But I tell you, Do not swear at all: either by heaven, for it is God's throne; or by the earth, for it is his footstool; or by Jerusalem, for it is the city of the Great King. And do not swear by your head, for you cannot make even one hair white or black. Simply let your 'Yes' be 'Yes,' and your 'No,' 'No'; anything beyond this comes from the evil one."

Matthew 5:34-37

❧

You must not swear to a falsehood, thus bringing reproach upon the name of your God, for I am Jehovah.

Leviticus 19:12 TLB

❧

If only you would slay the wicked, O God! Away from me, you bloodthirsty men! They speak of you with evil intent; your adversaries misuse your name.

Psalm 139:19-20

Need a marriage counselor? I'm available.

—GOD

Let all bitterness, and wrath, and anger, and clamour, and evil speaking, be put away from you, with all malice: And be ye kind one to another, tenderhearted, forgiving one another, even as God for Christ's sake hath forgiven you.

Ephesians 4:31-32 KJV

*Wives, submit to your husbands as to the Lord.
Husbands, love your wives, just as Christ loved
the church and gave himself up for her.*

Ephesians 5:22,25

*The man should give his wife all that is her
right as a married woman, and the wife should
do the same for her husband: for a girl who
marries no longer has full right to her own
body, for her husband then has his rights to it,
too; and in the same way the husband no
longer has full right to his own body, for it
belongs also to his wife. So do not refuse these
rights to each other.*

1 Corinthians 7:3-5 TLB

*Honor marriage, and guard the sacredness of
sexual intimacy between wife and husband.
God draws a firm line against casual and
illicit sex.*

Hebrews 13:4 THE MESSAGE

Safe sex? It's called marriage.

—GOD

Marriage should be honored by all, and the marriage bed kept pure.

Hebrews 13:4

Run from sex sin. No other sin affects the body as this one does. When you sin this sin it is against your own body.

1 Corinthians 6:18 TLB

❧

Our bodies were not made for sexual immorality. They were made for the Lord, and the Lord cares about our bodies

1 Corinthians 6:13 NLT

❧

Keep yourselves from sexual promiscuity. Learn to appreciate and give dignity to your body, not abusing it, as is so common among those who know nothing of God.

1 Thessalonians 4:4-5 THE MESSAGE

Sleepless? A clear conscience is a great pillow.

—GOD

I will maintain my righteousness and never let go of it; my conscience will not reproach me as long as I live.

Job 27:6

It is necessary to submit to the authorities, not only because of possible punishment but also because of conscience.

Romans 13:5

The goal of this command is love, which comes from a pure heart and a good conscience and a sincere faith.

1 Timothy 1:5

Who is going to harm you if you are eager to do good? But even if you should suffer for what is right, you are blessed.

1 Peter 3:13-14

If you must have the last word, make it "Sorry."

—GOD

If you are angry, don't sin by nursing your grudge. Don't let the sun go down with you still angry—get over it quickly.

Ephesians 4:26 TLB

Love is patient, love is kind. It does not envy, it does not boast, it is not proud.

1 Corinthians 13:4

In humility consider others better than yourselves. Each of you should look not only to your own interests, but also to the interests of others.

Philippians 2:3-4

Let us therefore make every effort to do what leads to peace and to mutual edification.

Romans 14:19

Leggo your ego.
—GOD

*Pride goes before destruction, a
haughty spirit before a fall.*

Proverbs 16:18

"Everyone who exalts himself will be humbled, and he who humbles himself will be exalted."

Luke 18:14 NKJV

❧

Pride leads to arguments; be humble, take advice and become wise.

Proverbs 13:10 TLB

❧

Do not think of yourself more highly than you should. Instead, be modest in your thinking.

Romans 12:3 TEV

Have you read my top 10 list lately?

—GOD

Fear God and keep his commandments, for this is the whole duty of man.

Ecclesiastes 12:13

"He who has my commandments and keeps them, he it is who loves me; and he who loves me will be loved by my Father, and I will love him and manifest myself to him."

John 14:21 RSV

"When you obey me you are living in my love, just as I obey my Father and live in his love."

John 15:10 TLB

It is the LORD your God you must follow, and him you must revere. Keep his commands and obey him; serve him and hold fast to him.

Deuteronomy 13:4

No one ever choked on swallowed pride.

—GOD

*A man's pride brings him
low, but a man of lowly spirit
gains honor.*

Proverbs 29:23

The patient in spirit is better than the proud in spirit.

Ecclesiastes 7:8 NKJV

When pride comes, then comes disgrace, but with humility comes wisdom.

Proverbs 11:2

To fear the LORD is to hate evil; I hate pride and arrogance, evil behavior and perverse speech.

Proverbs 8:13

Read the Bible and prevent truth decay.

—GOD

The whole Bible was given to us by inspiration from God and is useful to teach us what is true and to make us realize what is wrong in our lives.

2 Timothy 3:16 TLB

For the word of God is quick, and powerful, and sharper than any two-edged sword, piercing even to the dividing asunder of soul and spirit, and of the joints and marrow, and is a discerner of the thoughts and intents of the heart.

Hebrews 4:12 KJV

Thy word have I hid in mine heart, that I might not sin against thee. I will delight myself in thy statutes: I will not forget thy word.

Psalm 119:11,16 KJV

"Sanctify them through thy truth; thy word is truth."

John 17:17 KJV

Flee temptation— and don't leave a forwarding address.

—GOD

"Get up and pray so that you will not fall into temptation."

Luke 22:46

People are tempted when their own evil desire leads them away and traps them.

James 1:14 NCV

❧

If sinners entice you, turn your back on them!

Proverbs 1:10 NLT

❧

No temptation has overtaken you but such as is common to man; and God is faithful, who will not allow you to be tempted beyond what you are able, but with the temptation will provide the way of escape also, that you may be able to endure it.

1 Corinthians 10:13 NASB

What are you doing for the rest of your life?

—GOD

Let thine heart keep my commandments. For length of days, and long life, and peace, shall they add to thee.

Proverbs 3:1,2 KJV

With long life will I satisfy him, and shew him my salvation.

Psalm 91:16 KJV

Even to your old age I am he; and even to hoar hairs will I carry you: I have made, and I will bear; even I will carry, and will deliver you.

Isaiah 46:4 KJV

O God, thou hast taught me from my youth: and hitherto have I declared thy wondrous works. Now also when I am old and greyheaded, O God, forsake me not; until I have shewed thy strength unto this generation, and thy power to every one that is to come.

Psalm 71:17-18 KJV

OK, break it up!
—GOD

Love does no harm to a neighbor; therefore love is the fulfillment of the law.

Romans 13:10 NKJV

Stay on good terms with each other, held together by love.

Hebrews 13:1 THE MESSAGE

❧

"A new command I give you: Love one another."

John 13:34

❧

Let all bitterness, and wrath, and anger, and clamour, and evil speaking, be put away from you, with all malice: And be ye kind one to another, tenderhearted, forgiving one another, even as God for Christ's sake hath forgiven you.

Ephesians 4:31-32 KJV

They're commandments, not suggestions.
—GOD

"If you love me, you will obey what I command."

John 14:15

Fear God and keep his commandments, for this is the whole duty of man.

Ecclesiastes 12:13

"He who has my commandments and keeps them, he it is who loves me; and he who loves me will be loved by my Father, and I will love him and manifest myself to him."

John 14:21 RSV

"When you obey me you are living in my love, just as I obey my Father and live in his love."

John 15:10 TLB

God's
Eternal Love

I love you. I love you. I love you.

—GOD

For the mountains may depart and the hills be removed, but my steadfast love shall not depart from you, and my covenant of peace shall not be removed, says the LORD, who has compassion on you.

Isaiah 54:10 RSV

"God so loved the world that he gave his one and only Son, that whoever believes in him shall not perish but have eternal life."

John 3:16

It is because of the Lord's mercy and loving-kindness that we are not consumed, because His [tender] compassions fail not. They are new every morning; great and abundant is Your stability and faithfulness.

Lamentations 3:22-23 AMP

God demonstrates his own love for us in this: While we were still sinners, Christ died for us.

Romans 5:8

That "Love Thy Neighbor" thing . . . I meant that.

—GOD

If you really fulfill the royal law, according to the scripture, "You shall love your neighbor as yourself," you do well.

James 2:8 RSV

Serve one another in love. The entire law is summed up in a single command: "Love your neighbor as yourself." If you keep on biting and devouring each other, watch out or you will be destroyed by each other.

Galatians 5:13-15

Jesus replied, "'Love the Lord your God with all your heart, soul, and mind.' This is the first and greatest commandment. The second most important is similar: 'Love your neighbor as much as you love yourself.' All the other commandments and all the demands of the prophets stem from these two laws and are fulfilled if you obey them. Keep only these and you will find that you are obeying all the others."

Matthew 22:37-40 TLB

Stay on good terms with each other, held together by love.

Hebrews 13:1 THE MESSAGE

Some things break my heart too.

—GOD

*If you spend yourselves in behalf
of the hungry and satisfy the
needs of the oppressed, then your
light will rise in the darkness,
and your night will become like
the noonday.*

Isaiah 58:10

When *the poor and needy seek water, and*
there is *none,* and *their tongue faileth for
thirst,* I the L<small>ORD</small> *will hear them,* I the God of
Israel *will not forsake them.*

Isaiah 41:17 K<small>JV</small>

*He will deliver the needy who cry out, the
afflicted who have no one to help.*

Psalm 72:12

*"When you give a banquet, invite the poor, the
crippled, the lame, the blind, and you will be
blessed. Although they cannot repay you, you
will be repaid at the resurrection of the righteous."*

Luke 14:13-14

You're precious to me!

—GOD

Since you are precious and honored in my sight, and because I love you, I will give men in exchange for you, and people in exchange for your life.

Isaiah 43:4

"Are not two sparrows sold for a penny? Yet not one of them will fall to the ground apart from the will of your Father. And even the very hairs of your head are all numbered. So don't be afraid; you are worth more than many sparrows."

Matthew 10:29-31

For you created my inmost being; you knit me together in my mother's womb. I praise you because I am fearfully and wonderfully made; your works are wonderful, I know that full well.

Psalm 139:13-14

Can a mother forget the baby at her breast and have no compassion on the child she has borne? Though she may forget, I will not forget you! See, I have engraved you on the palms of my hands; your walls are ever before me.

Isaiah 49:15-16

When I said, "I love you," did you believe me?

—GOD

The LORD appeared to us in the past, saying: "I have loved you with an everlasting love; I have drawn you with loving-kindness."

Jeremiah 31:3

Because of his great love for us, God, who is rich in mercy, made us alive with Christ even when we were dead in transgressions.

Ephesians 2:4-5

The LORD is gracious and compassionate, slow to anger and rich in love.

Psalm 145:8

Because of the LORD's great love we are not consumed, for his compassions never fail. They are new every morning; great is your faithfulness.

Lamentations 3:22-23

Have you told me lately that you love me?

—GOD

Because he loves me," says the
LORD, "I will rescue him; I will
protect him, for he acknowledges
my name."

Psalm 91:14

"Do you love me? . . . Feed my sheep."

John 21:17

❧

This is love for God: to obey his commands. And his commands are not burdensome.

1 John 5:3

❧

Love the LORD *your God, listen to his voice, and hold fast to him. For the* LORD *is your life.*

Deuteronomy 30:20

I don't play favorites.

—GOD

[God] is not partial to princes, nor does He regard the rich more than the poor, for they all are the work of His hands.

Job 34:19 AMP

*Now let the fear of the LORD be upon you.
Judge carefully, for with the LORD our God there
is no injustice or partiality or bribery.*

2 Chronicles 19:7

❧

*I will show partiality to no one, nor will I flatter
any man.*

Job 32:21

❧

*For the LORD your God is God of gods and Lord
of lords, the great God, mighty and awesome,
who shows no partiality and accepts no bribes.*

Deuteronomy 10:17

Red, brown, yellow, black, and white— they are precious in my sight.

—GOD

Accept one another, then, just as Christ accepted you, in order to bring praise to God.

Romans 15:7

I will show partiality to no one, nor will I flatter any man.

Job 32:21

In humility consider others better than yourselves. Each of you should look not only to your own interests, but also to the interests of others.

Philippians 2:3-4

Let us therefore make every effort to do what leads to peace and to mutual edification.

Romans 14:19

Just where is this relationship going, anyway?
—GOD

Now, dear children, continue in him, so that when he appears we may be confident and unashamed before him at his coming.

1 John 2:28

Study to shew thyself approved unto God, a workman that needeth not to be ashamed, rightly dividing the word of truth.

2 Timothy 2:15 KJV

~

Being confident of this very thing, that he which hath begun a good work in you will perform it until the day of Jesus Christ.

Philippians 1:6 KJV

~

But grow in grace, and in the knowledge of our Lord and Saviour Jesus Christ. To him be glory both now and for ever. Amen.

2 Peter 3:18 KJV

Just say grace.
—GOD

By grace are ye saved through faith; and that not of yourselves: it is *the gift of God.*

Ephesians 2:8 KJV

God is able to make all grace abound to you, so that in all things at all times, having all that you need, you will abound in every good work.

2 Corinthians 9:8

The God of all grace, who called you to his eternal glory in Christ, after you have suffered a little while, will himself restore you and make you strong, firm and steadfast.

1 Peter 5:10

Grace and peace be yours in abundance through the knowledge of God and of Jesus our Lord.

2 Peter 1:2

Love one another. Is that so hard?
—GOD

Dear friends, let us love one another, for love comes from God.

1 John 4:7

Above all, love each other deeply, because love covers over a multitude of sins.

1 Peter 4:8

❧

Whoever loves is a child of God and knows God. Whoever does not love does not know God, for God is love.

1 John 4:7-8 TEV

❧

Those who do not love their brothers and sisters, whom they have seen, cannot love God, whom they have never seen.

1 John 4:20 NCV

Smile—I love you!
—GOD

The LORD your God is with you, he is mighty to save. He will take great delight in you, he will quiet you with his love, he will rejoice over you with singing.

Zephaniah 3:17

The LORD appeared to us in the past, saying: "I have loved you with an everlasting love; I have drawn you with loving-kindness."

Jeremiah 31:3

God demonstrates his own love for us in this: While we were still sinners, Christ died for us.

Romans 5:8

The LORD is gracious and compassionate, slow to anger and rich in love.

Psalm 145:8

The Ultimate Choice

Will the road you're on get you to my place?

—GOD

Nothing impure will ever enter it [heaven], nor will anyone who does what is shameful or deceitful, but only those whose names are written in the Lamb's book of life.

Revelation 21:27

*In keeping with his promise we are looking
forward to a new heaven and a new earth, the
home of righteousness. So then, dear friends,
since you are looking forward to this, make
every effort to be found spotless, blameless and
at peace with him.*

2 Peter 3:13-14

❧

*And now, my little children, stay in happy
fellowship with the Lord so that when he comes
you will be sure that all is well, and will not
have to be ashamed and shrink back from
meeting him.*

1 John 2:28 TLB

❧

*Behold, I am coming soon, and I shall bring My
wages* and *rewards with Me, to repay* and
*render to each one just what his own actions
and his own work merit. I am the Alpha and
the Omega, the First and the Last (the Before
all and the End of all). Blessed (happy and to
be envied) are those who cleanse their
garments, that they may have the authority* and
*right to [approach] the tree of life and to enter
through the gates into the city.*

Revelation 22:12-14 AMP

I don't take your name in vain.

—GOD

*You created my inmost being;
you knit me together in my
mother's womb. I praise you
because I am fearfully and
wonderfully made.*

Psalm 139:13-14

For he chose us in him before the creation of the world to be holy and blameless in his sight.

Ephesians 1:4

God has made us what we are. In Christ Jesus, God made us to do good works, which God planned in advance for us to live our lives doing.

Ephesians 2:10 NCV

He who overcomes will, like them, be dressed in white. I will never blot out his name from the book of life, but will acknowledge his name before my Father and his angels.

Revelation 3:5

Live for me;
I died for you.
—GOD

I have swept away your offenses like a cloud, your sins like the morning mist. Return to me, for I have redeemed you.

Isaiah 44:22

"He who believes in me will live, even though he dies; and whoever lives and believes in me will never die."

John 11:25-26

❧

We were therefore buried with him through baptism into death in order that, just as Christ was raised from the dead through the glory of the Father, we too may live a new life.

Romans 6:4

❧

Love the LORD your God, listen to his voice, and hold fast to him. For the LORD is your life.

Deuteronomy 30:20

When it comes to eternity, three things matter: location, location, location.

—GOD

Now we know that if the earthly tent we live in is destroyed, we have a building from God, an eternal house in heaven, not built by human hands.

2 Corinthians 5:1

"What good will it be for a man if he gains the whole world, yet forfeits his soul?"

Matthew 16:26

∾

Blessed are those who wash their robes, that they may have the right to the tree of life and may go through the gates into the city.

Revelation 22:14

∾

"In my Father's house are many rooms; if it were not so, I would have told you. I am going there to prepare a place for you."

John 14:2

Got questions?
I'm the answer.
—GOD

If any of you needs wisdom, you should ask God for it. He is generous and enjoys giving to all people, so he will give you wisdom.

James 1:5 NCV

*Praise be to the name of God for ever and ever;
wisdom and power are his. He reveals deep and
hidden things; he knows what lies in darkness,
and light dwells with him.*

Daniel 2:20,22

❧

*I [the Lord] will instruct you and teach you in
the way you should go; I will counsel you and
watch over you.*

Psalm 32:8

❧

*The LORD grants wisdom! His every word is a
treasure of knowledge and understanding.*

Proverbs 2:6 TLB

Going my way?
—GOD

There is a way which seemeth
right unto a man, but the end
thereof are *the ways of death.*

Proverbs 14:12 KJV

"Small is the gate and narrow the road that leads to life, and only a few find it."

Matthew 7:14

❧

As for God, his way is perfect; the word of the LORD is tried: he is a buckler to all them that trust in him.

2 Samuel 22:31 KJV

❧

Whether you turn to the right or to the left, your ears will hear a voice behind you, saying, "This is the way; walk in it."

Isaiah 30:21

Hell: Don't go there.

—GOD

The wicked shall be turned into hell, and *all the nations that forget God.*

Psalm 9:17 KJV

But the heavens and the earth, which are now, by the same word are kept in store, reserved unto fire against the day of judgment and perdition of ungodly men.

2 Peter 3:7 KJV

And death and hell were cast into the lake of fire. This is the second death. And whosoever was not found written in the book of life was cast into the lake of fire.

Revelation 20:14-15 KJV

"The subjects of the kingdom will be thrown outside, into the darkness, where there will be weeping and gnashing of teeth."

Matthew 8:12

It's getting dark—time to come home.
—GOD

"Keep watch, because you do not know on what day your Lord will come."

Matthew 24:42

"No one knows about that day or hour, not even the angels in heaven, nor the Son, but only the Father."

Mark 13:32

❧

"Take ye heed, watch and pray: for ye know not when the time is."

Mark 13:33 KJV

❧

The day of the Lord will come like a thief. The heavens will disappear with a roar; the elements will be destroyed by fire, and the earth and everything in it will be laid bare.

2 Peter 3:10

Got me?

—GOD

Those who know your name will trust in you, for you, LORD, have never forsaken those who seek you.

Psalm 9:10

"I give unto them eternal life; and they shall never perish, neither shall any man pluck them out of my hand."

John 10:28 KJV

We say with confidence, "The Lord is my helper; I will not be afraid. What can man do to me?"

Hebrews 13:6

I will put my Spirit in you and you will live.

Ezekiel 37:14

Need directions?
—GOD

*For this God is our God for ever
and ever: he will be our guide
even unto death.*

Psalm 48:14 KJV

Trust in the LORD with all your heart and lean not on your own understanding; in all your ways acknowledge him, and he will make your paths straight.

Proverbs 3:5-6

If I rise on the wings of the dawn, if I settle on the far side of the sea, even there your hand will guide me, your right hand will hold me fast.

Psalm 139:9-10

I guide you in the way of wisdom and lead you along straight paths.

Proverbs 4:11

You think it's hot here?
—GOD

"God did not send his Son into the world to condemn the world, but to save the world through him."

John 3:17

The wicked shall be turned into hell, and *all the nations that forget God.*

Psalm 9:17 KJV

But the heavens and the earth which are now, by the same word are kept in store, reserved unto fire against the day of judgment and perdition of ungodly men.

2 Peter 3:7 KJV

And death and hell were cast into the lake of fire. This is the second death. And whosoever was not found written in the book of life was cast into the lake of fire.

Revelation 20:14-15 KJV

I'm the only one who really knows what time it is.

—GOD

"No one knows about that day or hour, not even the angels in heaven, nor the Son, but only the Father."

Mark 13:32

*For what man knoweth the things of a man,
save the spirit of man which is in him? even so
the things of God knoweth no man, but the
Spirit of God.*

1 Corinthians 2:11 KJV

*"Take ye heed, watch and pray: for ye know not
when the time is."*

Mark 13:33 KJV

*The day of the Lord will come like a thief. The
heavens will disappear with a roar; the elements
will be destroyed by fire, and the earth and
everything in it will be laid bare.*

2 Peter 3:10

Believe me now.
See me later.
—GOD

"I tell you the truth, he who believes has everlasting life."

John 6:47

Jesus said to her, "I am the resurrection and the life. He who believes in me will live, even though he dies; and whoever lives and believes in me will never die."

John 11:25-26

Whoever believes in the Son has eternal life.

John 3:36

"My sheep recognize my voice, and I know them, and they follow me. I give them eternal life and they shall never perish. No one shall snatch them away from me."

John 10:27-28 TLB

Dear One,

If this book has been a thought-provoking journey for you and you would like to learn more about Me, spend some time reading My Bible. Find one that speaks to you in your everyday language.

Most of all, I want to develop a relationship with you. Talk to Me, and listen to what I have to say. Join a Bible study group, and find a church where you can fellowship with other people who love Me. Ask lots of questions. Tell them you're new at this "God thing." They'll understand.

And remember . . . you are never alone. I am always with you.

Love,
GOD

Additional copies of this book and other
titles in the GodSpeaks™ series
are available at your local bookstore.

GodSpeaks™ Devotional
GodSpeaks™ Journal
GodSpeaks™ Stories for Teens

If you have enjoyed this book,
or if it has impacted your life,
we would like to hear from you.

Please contact us at:

Honor Books
Department E
P.O. Box 55388
Tulsa, Oklahoma 74155

Or by e-mail at info@honorbooks.com